W9-BSD-804

8/01

Photographers

by Fran Hodgkins

Consultant:
Glenn Melvin, M. Photog., Cr., ASP
Executive Manager
Professional Photographers' Society of New York, Inc.

Bridgestone Books
an imprint of Capstone Press
Mankato, Minnesota

Bridgestone Books are published by Capstone Press
151 Good Counsel Drive, P.O. Box 669, Mankato, Minnesota 56002
http://www.capstone-press.com

Library of Congress Cataloging-in-Publication Data
Hodgkins, Fran, 1964–
      Photographers/by Fran Hodgkins.
      p. cm.—(Community helpers)
      Includes bibliographical references and index.
      ISBN 0-7368-0809-4
      1. Photography—Vocational guidance—Juvenile literature. 2. Photographers—Juvenile
literature. [1. Photographers. 2. Occupations.] I. Title. II. Community helpers
(Mankato, Minn.)
TR154 .H64 2001
770' .23—dc21

                                                                                    00-009953

Summary: A simple introduction to the work photographers do, tools they use, skills they
      need, necessary schooling, and their importance to the communities they serve.

Editorial Credits
Sarah Lynn Schuette, editor; Karen Risch, product planning editor; Heather Kindseth, cover
      designer; Heidi Schoof, photo researcher

Photo Credits
GeoIMAGERY/J & D Richardson, 12
Index Stock Imagery/Raeanne Ruben, 10
International Stock/Dusty Willison, 4
Jim Cummins/FPG International LLC, cover
Llewellyn/Pictor, 18
Photo Network/Tom Tracy, 6
Richard Cummins, 8
Rob and Ann Simpson, 14
Unicorn Stock Photos/Gary L. Johnson, 16
Visuals Unlimited/Barry Slaven, 20

1 2 3 4 5 6 06 05 04 03 02 01

Table of Contents

Photographers

Photographers use cameras to take pictures. Some photographers are professionals. They are paid for the pictures they take. Photographers also take pictures for fun.

What Photographers Do

Photographers take pictures of people, nature, and news events. They set up backgrounds and models who pose for pictures. Many photographers develop their own film. Film records pictures in color or in black and white.

develop
to put chemicals on film to show a picture

Different Kinds of Photographers

Nature photographers often shoot pictures for newspapers, magazines, and books. Portrait photographers take pictures of people, families, and pets. Other photographers take pictures for police departments or hospitals.

Where Photographers Work

Many photographers work in studios.
A studio can be a room or a building.
Photographers often take pictures
at special events such as weddings.
They also travel to shoot pictures.
Some photographers develop film
in darkrooms.

Tools Photographers Use

Photographers use different kinds of cameras. Digital cameras record pictures to use on computers. Photographers also use light filters, flashes, and tripods. Light filters change the color and light in pictures. Flashes help make pictures brighter. Tripods hold cameras steady.

tripod
a stand with three legs

Skills Photographers Need

Photographers need to know how to use a camera correctly. They know how to focus a camera. They also know when to use a flash and a light filter. Photographers should be friendly to the people they photograph.

focus

to make pictures clear and not fuzzy

Photographers and School

Photographers can be any age. Some photography students go to college. Other people take community classes. All photography students learn how to take good pictures and develop film. They also learn about cameras.

college

a place where students study after high school

17

People Who Help Photographers

Photographer assistants help load film into cameras. They help photographers set up models. Assistants also develop film. Photo editors choose pictures to use in magazines, newspapers, and books.

assistant
a person who helps someone else do a job

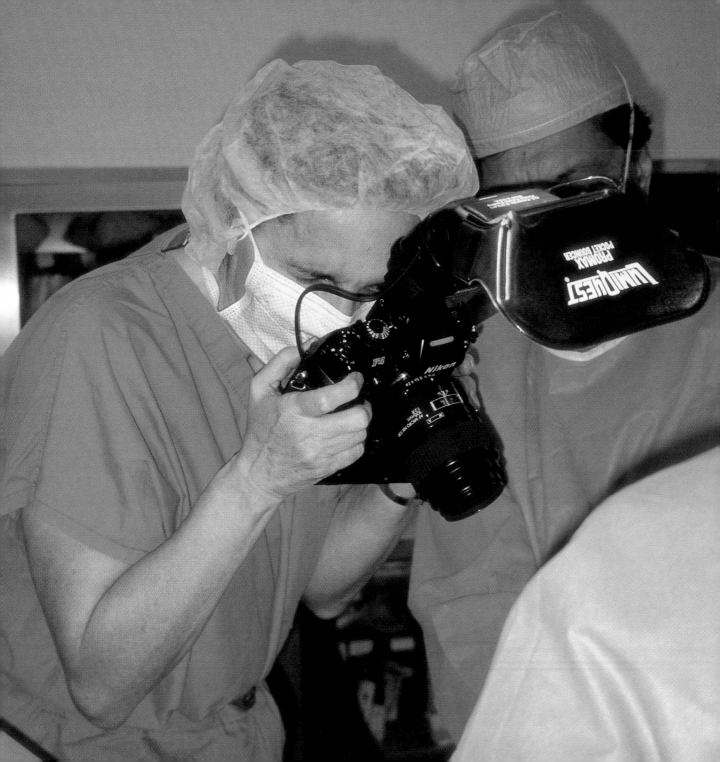

How Photographers Help Others

Photographers help to record events, objects, and people's lives. Medical pictures can save lives. Doctors often use these pictures to study injuries. Other pictures help solve crimes. Pictures sometimes help people remember the past.

injury
damage or harm
to the body

Hands On: Upside-Down Picture Box

Shoebox with a lid   Scissors
Black paint   Tape
An adult   Wax paper
Ruler   Markers

What You Do

1. Paint the inside of the shoebox and the lid black.
2. Ask an adult to cut an opening 2 inches by 2 inches
   (5 centimeters by 5 centimeters) in the middle of the small
   end of the box. Tape a piece of wax paper over the opening.
   Put the cover on the box.
3. Have the adult make a small hole with the scissor in the
   opposite end of the box. This hole will let light into the box.
4. Decorate your picture box with markers. Take the picture
   box outside and look through the wax paper at an object.
   How does it look?

The object you see should be upside down. The light bounces
off the inside of the box and reflects the object to your eye
upside down. Camera lenses reflect upside-down pictures to
make them look right side up.

Words to Know

background (BAK-ground)—the setting behind the main subject of a picture

digital camera (DIJ-uh-tuhl KAM-ur-uh)—a camera that records pictures to use on computers

film (FILM)—a roll of thin plastic; film records pictures in color or in black and white.

model (MOD-uhl)—someone who poses for a picture

professional (pruh-FESH-uh-nuhl)—someone who is paid to do a job

studio (STOO-dee-oh)—a room or building in which a photographer works

tripod (TRYE-pod)—a stand with three legs; tripods hold cameras steady.

Read More

Gibbons, Gail. *Click!: A Book about Cameras and Taking Pictures.* Boston: Little, Brown, 1997.

Graham, Ian. *Film and Photography.* Communications Close-up. Austin, Tex.: Raintree Steck-Vaughn, 2000.

Quinlan, Kathryn A. *Photographer.* Careers without College. Mankato, Minn.: Capstone Books, 1999.

Internet Sites

Photographer
http://stats.bls.gov:80/k12/html/mus_003.htm
Photographer Page
http://www.webquarry.com/~lgfd/photogra.htm

Index